YOUR DIVINE DESIGN

HOW TO DISCOVER, DEVELOP, AND DEPLOY YOUR SPIRITUAL GIFTS

CHIPINGRAM

Living on the Edge
© 2022 by Chip Ingram and Living on the Edge

P.O. Box 3007, Suwanee, GA 30024
www.livingontheedge.org

ISBN: 978-1-60593-469-3

All Scripture quotations in this publication are taken from the Holy Bible, New International Version®, NIV®. Copyright ©1973, 1978, 1984, 2011 by Biblica, Inc.® Used by permission of Zondervan. All rights reserved worldwide. www.Zondervan.com

Printed in the United States

Y⬤UR DIVINE DESIGN

HOW TO DISCOVER, DEVELOP, AND DEPLOY YOUR SPIRITUAL GIFTS

CONTENTS

INTRODUCTION

Jim lived in Alaska but did a lot of business in California. That business was cocaine. He was a drug dealer, an addict, and an alcoholic. His family was falling apart, and his life was a wreck.

Then Jim came to Christ, and his life began to change, miraculously. He and his wife moved to Northern California. He got work as a janitor, stayed sober, began to read the Bible, and started coming to our church. Thanks largely to my wife's gift of mercy and her sensitivity to people's needs, Jim got more involved. Our family pastor and some small-group leaders invested time with him, and God's Word took deeper root in his heart and mind.

Jim began to ask what God wanted him to do with his life. After discovering his spiritual gifts, he began a recovery ministry. It grew into the largest of its kind in Northern California. He knew what addicts went through, and he knew how to care for and challenge them. Most importantly, he knew how to guide them toward a relationship with Christ. He attended college and became a pastor, speaking all over the country to people struggling with substance abuse. Jim's adult son came to visit and wondered how this man could be the father he knew growing up.

Jim is a dramatic example of an extreme makeover—a drug-dealer-turned-janitor-turned-minister whose life went from a disastrous wreck to a beautiful picture of redeeming grace and miraculous fruitfulness.

Extreme Makeovers

We all love a good makeover, don't we? For decades, television's most popular offerings have been shows that give viewers a front-row seat to the transformation of houses, cars, restaurants, people, and just about anything else in need of a radical makeover. The process of taking something old, broken, imperfect, or no longer useful and turning it into something useful, beautiful, new, and whole is fascinating. When the finished product is unveiled, jaws drop and tears flow. It's an exciting moment.

Why are we so fascinated by such transformations? For one thing, we love to see positive change. Another reason is our curiosity about how it happens—the skill and creativity involved in making the old new, the broken whole, and the unappealing beautiful. But I think the main reason we find makeovers fascinating is that we all want one. Deep down, we long for change—not just gradual change but radical transformation. We want to be different.

God designed us that way. He is the Author of extreme makeovers and has written that desire into our spiritual DNA. It's our story. Jesus Christ working in a human heart takes what is old, broken, imperfect, or no longer useful in our lives and turns us into something useful, beautiful, new, and whole.

The apostle Paul expressed this perfectly: "If anyone is in Christ, the new creation has come: The old has gone, the new is here!" (2 Corinthians 5:17). God wants that for every human being on the planet. He wants to transform us into something and someone wonderful.

The Ultimate Makeover

The second chapter of Ephesians gives us a clear picture of the ultimate makeover. The passage presents the kind of before-and-after contrast that brings tears to people's eyes. Here's the "before" of our lives:

> You were dead in your transgressions and sins, in which you used to live when you followed the ways of this world and of the ruler of the

kingdom of the air, the spirit who is now at work in those who are disobedient. All of us also lived among them at one time, gratifying the cravings of our flesh and following its desires and thoughts. Like the rest, we were by nature deserving of wrath. (verses 1-3)

That's a human life in need of renovation—or, in this case, a resurrection. We were dead in sin, separated from God, prisoners of the world's system and all its dysfunctional relationships, and addicted to our own cravings, manipulation, and people-pleasing habits.

That's who we were, but by the grace of God, we've been given a completely different "after" picture:

Because of his great love for us, God, who is rich in mercy, made us alive with Christ even when we were dead in transgressions—it is by grace you have been saved. And God raised us up with Christ and seated us with him in the heavenly realms in Christ Jesus. (verses 4-6)

We who were dead are now alive. We who were prisoners are now delivered from sin's power, Satan's grip, past mistakes, and the curse of death. We who were once objects of wrath now have a new standing with God as righteous and clean. We have a new identity, a new power, a new future, a new purpose, new privileges, and a new inheritance. It's the most dramatic, extreme makeover ever.

Why did God do this? What was His motivation for making such a radical change happen?

> [He did this] in order that in the coming ages he might show the incomparable riches of his grace, expressed in his kindness to us in Christ Jesus. For it is by grace you have been saved, through faith—and this is not from yourselves, it is the gift of God—not by works, so that no one can boast. (verses 7-9)

God wants to demonstrate the riches of His grace. This whole makeover is a revelation of His nature— His goodness, kindness, compassion, love, wisdom, and power. He puts His people on display to exhibit what He is really like so human beings can know Him.

That's what Jim's story—and the story of many others—accomplishes. When I look at where Jim was compared to where

> God puts His people on display to exhibit what He is really like.

he ended up, I'm amazed at everything that happened between "before" and "after."

His story also demonstrates how God uses special passions and abilities He gives us in this ultimate makeover process. The apostle Paul called these "spiritual gifts." God took the spiritual gift of mercy in my wife, Theresa, to make Jim feel loved at a time when he didn't think anyone cared.

Through my and others' spiritual gift of teaching in our congregation, God replaced lies Jim believed about his identity with the truth of God's Word.

God used the exhortation of one of our counselors to help Jim learn and grow. He used the spiritual gifts of a small-group community to demonstrate His love, kindness, and acceptance.

Jim saw that he had spiritual gifts too and began to reproduce in the lives of others what God was doing in his life. He experienced the joy and fulfillment of being fruitful in God's Kingdom, and through him, many others also experienced joy and fulfillment.

Just like He did in Jim's life, God wants to put away the old in your life and replace it with the new. He wants an open door in your heart and life through which to give you new desires, purpose, peace, and fruitfulness. His extreme makeover has brought you into a relationship with Jesus in order to shape you into His image. And, as you'll discover, the spiritual gifts His Spirit has placed in you make the "after" of your life a beautifully fulfilling picture for all to see.

(1)

A MASTERPIECE
in the Making

You are a masterpiece in the making.

The extreme makeover God is taking you through
is not just a cosmetic upgrade or self-improvement
program, and it isn't about only you. If you had any
doubts about that, notice where the first nine verses
of Ephesians 2 have been leading:

> We are God's handiwork, created in Christ
> Jesus to do good works, which God prepared
> in advance for us to do. (verse 10)

That word *handiwork* (or workmanship in some translations) conveys a masterpiece, a work of the finest craftsmanship. When you become a new creation in Christ (2 Corinthians 5:17), you are given a renewed purpose and are being handcrafted by God to fulfill it. He is giving you a second (or third or hundredth) chance to become the person He originally designed you to be: your divine design. He is an artist painting you as a beautiful piece of art, or a sculptor shaping you into a remarkable sculpture, or a literary genius writing a profoundly fulfilling and meaningful story with your life.

Ephesians 2:10 not only identifies what God is doing in your life but also tells you how and why. His master workmanship is recreating you through your relationship with Christ for the purpose of doing good works.

Deep down, we all want a sense of purpose, don't we? Think of Rick Warren's *The Purpose Driven Life*, which, although first published two decades ago in 2002, remains a best-selling Christian book. It wouldn't have sold more than 50 million copies in various formats in over 137 languages if the human heart weren't filled with a hunger for meaning and purpose.

No surprise, then, that God tells us right there in Ephesians 2:10 what His purpose for us is. It's to do the works He puts in front of us to do.

Before the foundation of the world, God knew you and loved you (Ephesians 1:3-5). He saved you, understands you, cares for you, and wants to restore to you all His good purposes for your life. To do that, He is calling you to put away the old nature, maintain a deep relationship with Christ, and demonstrate His goodness, wisdom, and love. That's what the makeover is all about: your life becoming beautiful, winsome, and kind—an illustration of God's very nature.

As a means toward that end, God planned good works and purposes specifically for you to fulfill.

Not only that, but He designed you so that you'd be able to do what He planned for you. And as you'll see in the following pages, He equipped you with the gifts and tools you need.

That's how it worked with my friend Jim. God preordained that He would rescue and restore Jim and then give him the gifts to reach into people's lives to help *them*. First it was drug addicts, then alcoholics, then sex offenders, and on and on. It kept building as Jim allowed the love and grace of Christ to pour through his life into the lives of many others.

God wants to do something like that in each of us. It will look different from person to person, but the goal is the same. You are a special masterpiece designed to demonstrate the nature of the Artist who made you.

The Master's Studio

This doesn't just happen spontaneously, though. There is a step-by-step process made possible because of what Christ did on the cross, providing us "access to the Father by one Spirit" (Ephesians 2:18). Paul went on to write about the essential context in which the Master Craftsman does His work in us:

> You are no longer foreigners and strangers, but fellow citizens with God's people and also *members of his household*, built on the foundation of the apostles and prophets, with Christ Jesus himself as the chief cornerstone. In him *the whole building is joined together* and rises to become *a holy temple* in the Lord. And in him *you too are being built together to become a dwelling in which God lives* by his Spirit. (verses 19-22, emphasis added)

Notice the italicized phrases; this is a household, a temple, a joining together of believers in Jesus to be inhabited by God's Spirit. Paul presents a picture of all who are in Christ being built together into God's dwelling place.

In other words, God does spiritual makeovers in a special place: in a supernatural community we call the Church. That's where the old becomes new— where unshaped clay is turned into a magnificent sculpture in the Master's hands.

> **The Church is the Craftsman's studio where masterpieces are made.**

When the New Testament talks about the Church, it is not describing a building or institutional religion. It's talking about the living, breathing, called-out people of God who are living in community together, walking authentically and faithfully, doing life together in the power of the Holy Spirit based on God's Word. The Church is the Craftsman's studio where masterpieces are made.

That's why local churches are the hope of the world. Some may be operating in a dysfunctional manner, missing out on the makeovers God wants to do, but that doesn't negate His original purpose. Christ-centered communities are still where He redeems, restores, and renews people so they can live out their callings in the world. When God's people gather around His Word and are empowered by His Spirit, lives change.

A few verses later in Ephesians, we see the larger purpose:

> His intent was that now, through the church, the manifold wisdom of God should be made known to the rulers and authorities in the heavenly realms, according to his eternal purpose that he accomplished in Christ Jesus our Lord. (3:10-11)

God's overarching plan was for His people to become demonstrations of His wisdom and character so the entire universe could see the amazing makeovers that God's grace and power produce. When all the people on earth, as well as the "great cloud of witnesses" (Hebrews 12:1) in heaven, see someone like Jim reach out to restore sex addicts and substance abusers, they marvel at God's greatness. That kind of radical change demonstrates God's "manifold wisdom"—His unmatchable knowledge and skill.

We notice when a person's outward appearance is completely remade by fashion and makeup artists. We're impressed when designers and contractors renovate a house into something better than we could have imagined. That takes vision and skill. But when human beings are remade from being "dead in [their] transgressions and sins" (Ephesians 2:1) into trophies of God's grace, the whole universe is in awe.

God wants every human being on planet Earth to see what He does in His people and think, *Wow!* When He reveals the beauty and glory of His nature through the demonstrations of wisdom, power, and love in His Church, He wants us to realize, *Lord, You're so much more wonderful, powerful, faithful, and loving than I could have dreamed.*

Heart-to-Heart Transformation

That's the corporate, communal side of things.
But there's also an individual, internal side. God
does extreme makeovers in two places: *in the
Church*, which He is building up as His dwelling
place, and *in the human heart*, which He is
aligning with His heart.

Paul prayed that the Holy Spirit would empower
believers so that we in faith would experience the
indwelling in our hearts of Christ Himself, all for
His larger purposes:

> I pray that out of his glorious riches he may
> strengthen you with power through his Spirit
> in your inner being, so that Christ may dwell
> in your hearts through faith. And I pray that
> you, being rooted and established in love, may
> have power, together with all the Lord's holy
> people, to grasp how wide and long and high
> and deep is the love of Christ, and to know this

love that surpasses knowledge—that you may
be filled to the measure of all the fullness of
God. (Ephesians 3:16-19)

Every human being who allows the Spirit of God
to have His way in his or her heart becomes a
demonstration to the world of God's wisdom. It
isn't magic; you don't just walk into a room, get
transformed, and come out a new person. It is
supernatural, and it happens in a supernatural
community where His Spirit dwells.

Your DNA is unique, physically and spiritually.
God loves you, saved you, and called you
individually. He has a unique purpose for you and
has laid out good works for you to do that no one
else can. Those may be high-profile or behind-the-
scenes works, but they are yours and only yours.
And you are being prepared for these good works
in the depths of your heart and in the community
of believers.

How the Masterpiece Is Made

The first part of Ephesians presents the new you. The first three chapters show the extreme makeover God does in every believer's life, a transformation He had planned even before He created the world. Ephesians 2, as we have seen, was largely about the who and what— what you used to be like and who you are now. Ephesians 3 was about the why— God's purpose in it all.

That brings us to Ephesians 4, where the message now shifts from our identity in Christ to our life in Him. It turns to the process and how it works. Now that we are loved, adopted, and accepted by the Father, redeemed and transformed in Christ, and sealed with the Spirit, what does this new life look like?

Ephesians 4 opens with a challenge to live out what we now know to be true. In other words, since God has done all these miraculous, wonderful things and we already possess them, we are to walk in a manner

"worthy of the calling" (verse 1). What we believe
and how we live ought to line up.

That can happen only when we embrace the
nature and character of God (verses 2-6) and
receive the gifts He has given us (verses 7-13).
We each have been endowed with grace (verse
7). It's an endowment, a share in the plunder of
Christ's victory over sin and death (verse 8). Paul is
evoking an image of a conquering king completely
stripping his enemy of power and giving the
spoils of war to his fellow warriors. He casts it as
a cosmic battle that fills the universe with Christ's
glory; the gifts that come from this victory are
therefore otherworldly gifts (verses 9-10). They are
supernatural.

With that in mind, notice how these gifts operate in
the lives of Christians and the Church:

> Christ himself gave the apostles, the prophets,
> the evangelists, the pastors and teachers, to
> equip his people for works of service, so that

the Body of Christ may be built up until
we all reach unity in the faith and in the
knowledge of the Son of God and become
mature, attaining to the whole measure of the
fullness of Christ. (verses 11-13)

When Jesus died on the cross for your sin, He
redeemed you. Restoration began when you put
your faith in Him. Between the time of His death
on the cross and His resurrection from the grave,
He proclaimed His victory over Satan, sin, and
death. That's how it's possible for you to have been
dead in sin (2:1) but now alive with Christ and
seated with Him in heavenly places (verses 5-6).
He broke the power of sin and death in your life.
And the evidence of this wonderful, miraculous
event is the spiritual gifts He gives to each and
every believer.

Those are our tools for transformation. Just as an
artist uses a paintbrush or a sculptor uses chisels and
detailing instruments, God uses spiritual gifts to
shape His human masterpieces.

> **Our task is to discover, develop, and deploy our spiritual gifts.**

As we live in an authentic, loving community centered around the Word of God and exercise our spiritual gifts, we become the paintbrushes and trowels in His hands. The results these gifts produce are evidence of Jesus's victory. They demonstrate that Satan, sin, and death have no power over us. Our task is to discover, develop, and deploy our spiritual gifts for God's purposes and our joy and fulfillment.

Gifts for Specific Purposes

If you're wondering why we've gone through so much of Ephesians to get to the main focus of this book—which is discovering, developing, and deploying spiritual gifts according to God's design for each of us—it's because many Christians approach spiritual gifts as though they are items on a buffet table. They consider the options, take a test that helps identify their interests, and pick one they would like to have.

Even though desires and tests can help us with
our understanding, spiritual gifts are not there
just for the choosing. God has given *specific
gifts* to each of His people to fulfill their *specific
purposes* (1 Corinthians 12:11).

God made each of us to be a tool in His hands,
and like physical tools, we aren't effective if we
aren't being used according to His design. I've
tried hammering with a screwdriver before, and it
doesn't work very well. Tools are useful only in the
situations they were made for.

Discovering the gifts that are ours is a process
that involves study, much prayer, and evidence of
fruitfulness. That may be why some Christians can't
say with certainty what their spiritual gifts are. Such
knowledge should be the basis of our life choices,
yet over and over again, as a lifelong pastor, I've
watched believers make crucial decisions without
that fundamental knowledge.

Realizing your specific gifts would likely spare you a lot of frustration. It would keep you from saying yes simply to fill a position when you really ought to say no. Too many faithful people have been manipulated by guilt into serving in areas where they are not gifted. Joy and fruitfulness are rarely the results. Of course, I understand that sometimes situations call for someone to step up and meet a need; you do what you have to do when the circumstances call for it. But it is never effective to operate in someone else's good works. Most of a person's time, energy, and focus should be invested in the areas of their God-given giftedness.

I did a lot of "Christian" things as a young believer because I thought more activity meant more fruitfulness. But my joy and the impact of my life for God's Kingdom never got off the ground until I got clear on what my spiritual gifts were and then focused my time and energy on them. When I learned to say no to possibilities that didn't fit those gifts, God began to use my life in ways I had never dreamed of. It had nothing to do with being special or earning His blessings. God was using the free gifts He had given me at the time of salvation to accomplish His purposes.

It's simply a matter of discovering the paintbrushes within us and learning how to use them to add our colors to the masterpieces God is creating in other people's hearts and lives. When we do that, the life of Christ becomes visible in us. The "manifold wisdom of God" (Ephesians 3:10) is on display.

Can you see how wisely using your spiritual gifts is so much more important than filling the slots at church each year to make sure all the programs are covered? The goal is not about keeping believers busy, getting them connected, or helping them become more productive. God is not aiming at moderate improvement; He wants an extreme makeover in your life and the lives of people who need to experience the spiritual gifts you've been given.

God wants an extreme makeover in your life.

Your spiritual gifts came into your life at the same time the Spirit of God came in: when you placed your faith in Christ. Whether you recognized any of the gifts then or not, they were there. And now the Master Artist wants them to color the masterpiece of His Kingdom. You are a paintbrush in His hands.

TEN PRINCIPLES FOR UNDERSTANDING SPIRITUAL GIFTS*

1. Every Christian has one or more spiritual gifts.

2. Many believers have received more than one spiritual gift.

3. Spiritual gifts are given at the moment of regeneration, but they may lie undiscovered and dormant for a long period of time.

4. Spiritual gifts can lie dormant or be neglected, but they cannot be lost.

5. Spiritual gifts are not the same as the gift of the Holy Spirit.

6. Spiritual gifts are not the same as the fruit of the Spirit.

7. Spiritual gifts are not the same as natural talents.

8. Some spiritual gifts are more useful in local churches than others because they result in greater edification of the body.

9. *Charismata* literally means "grace gifts." These gifts are sovereignly and undeservedly given by the Holy Spirit.

10. Spiritual gifts are God's spiritual equipment for effective service and edification of the body.

* See Romans 12; 1 Corinthians 12, 14; Ephesians 4; 1 Peter 4:10-11.

Questions to Ponder

- How have you understood spiritual gifts in the past?

- How did this chapter help clarify why God gives spiritual gifts?

- Look over the chart on the previous page. Do any of the principles surprise you? If so, which ones and why?

- Describe how God has used the spiritual gifts of others to help shape and transform your life.

2

Discovering
YOUR PRIMARY
SPIRITUAL GIFT

The Master Artist holds an infinite number of paintbrushes in His hand, with an endless array of colors on His palette—all the better for shaping us into the image of Jesus. Spiritual gifts are unique and diverse. Your gifts will look different from those given to others. Even those who have the same gifts as you will express them differently.

Some are precision instruments, delicately working God's detailed artistry into the lives of others. Some are like large brushes that paint broad strokes. Some are shaped in particular ways to enhance angles and textures, while others might as well be paint rollers that carry no individual touch but influence masses.

Don't waste time chasing after a spiritual gift you see in someone else. That's just not how it works. Focus on identifying and accepting how God has perfectly and wisely gifted you.

Based on biblical teachings, there's a good chance you have more than one spiritual gift, and perhaps two or three. One of them will be primary. It's important to know which one that is.

It might take a while to figure it out. For a long time, I didn't know what mine was. In fact, I can divide my life as it relates to spiritual gifts into four distinct eras.

A Process of Discovery

First was my "era of ignorance." I did not grow up as a Christian, so when I received Christ and began reading the New Testament, I was only vaguely aware of spiritual gifts as a concept. I had never heard any teaching on them; I just thought they were kind of an interesting idea that didn't really apply to me.

Then came my "era of confusion." After two or three years of being a Christian, I realized that whenever I heard people talking about spiritual gifts, they were usually disagreeing over which ones were permanent or temporary, which ones were essential for all believers or nonessential for anyone, and so on. The debates sort of paralyzed me. I figured that if the gifts produced that kind of dissension, I might not want any of them.

Then I went to seminary and eventually became a young pastor. I was in my "era of discovery." I immersed myself in the Bible. I did extensive word studies and came out with a lot of knowledge about etymologies and the biblical contexts in which all the various spiritual gifts appear.

I learned that every Christian has one or more spiritual gifts (1 Corinthians 12:11). They're not the same as natural talents, nor are they spiritual fruit. Rather, they are sovereignly bestowed by God as an act of grace. They are endowments for service, with their purpose being to build others up in the Body of Christ (1 Corinthians 12:7).

I also learned that spiritual gifts can lie dormant or be ignored if Christians do not learn about them or how to use them (2 Timothy 1:6; 1 Peter 4:10). But they cannot be lost. A believer can develop them at any point on his or her walk with Christ.

All these basic principles were very helpful, but I still had a big buffet of spiritual gifts in front of me without knowing exactly which ones God had put on my plate.

I eventually came to my "era of empowerment." I discovered which of my spiritual gifts is primary, the one that I call the ***motivational gift***, because it aligns with my most powerful spiritual passion.

Then I learned what other gifts were *ministry gifts* surrounding my ***motivational gift***. I began to make decisions about what to do with my life based on that ***motivational gift*** and focused my energy and time around it. It began to shape everything about me.

Understanding your ***motivational gift*** and how it fits with God's purposes for you is extremely empowering. You begin to live according to the way God made you and what He wants you to do. It brings clarity to your life.

> Understanding your motivational gift and how it fits with God's purpose for you is extremely empowering.

Spiritual Gifts in the New Testament

There are four major passages in the New Testament on spiritual gifts: Romans 12:4-8, 1 Corinthians 12, Ephesians 4:11-13, and 1 Peter 4:10-11. I suggest looking at these passages now and becoming familiar with them.

Different passages include different terms and in different contexts. Some of the lists of spiritual gifts overlap quite a bit. Sometimes they seem to be random collections and imply that the twenty-six or so spiritual gifts may or may not be comprehensive. Some, like those in Ephesians 4, relate to specific roles within the Church, and one (1 Peter 4) puts them in a really broad paradigm.

How to organize the gifts is a matter of debate, sometimes provoking the kind of dissension that turned me off in my "era of confusion." But I've found it to be very helpful to put them in some sort of framework so that they make sense.

There certainly are many valid ways to look at spiritual gifts, but I believe God has given believers a lens in 1 Corinthians 12 that shows how all the spiritual gifts fit together.

> There are different kinds of *gifts*, but the same Spirit distributes them. There are different kinds of *service*, but the same Lord. There are different kinds of *working*, but in all of them and in

everyone it is the same God at work. (verses 4-6, emphasis added)

The apostle Paul wrote these words to the church in Corinth, which seemed to have more spiritual gifts operating than any other church, but the people were confused about the gifts and misusing them. Paul's aim was to help them understand how the gifts fit together to serve, and how believers themselves fit together to form the Body of Christ.

You'll notice three categories in Paul's statement:

- "Different kinds of *gifts*" (motivational): The Greek word here is *charismata*, literally "grace gifts"—supernatural endowments from God.
- "Different kinds of *service*" (ministry): The term here is *diakonia*, from which we get "deacon" and simply means "a waiter of tables"—those who serve.
- "Different kinds of *working*" (manifestation):

The word here is *energematon*, which expresses the idea of "energy."

Paul acknowledged that some gifts function as **motivational gifts** that show up in our lives as passions or drives. These strong, motivational drives will play out in different arenas of service, which then energize or manifest the work of God's Spirit in the Body of Christ in various ways.

To summarize—and again, this is one helpful framework, not a rigid, definitive structure—there seem to be three categories of spiritual gifts, and I believe that every Christian has one primary gift that most motivates him or her. These **motivational gifts** are found in Romans 12:6-8. I believe we are to concentrate first and foremost on discovering and developing which of the seven we're gifted with.

Beyond this **motivational gift** are *ministry gifts* that are expressed through a variety of ministries. We see them in Ephesians 4:11-13 and 1 Corinthians 12:28-31.

And then there's a third category, the *manifestations* of the gifts. These show up when we exercise our **motivational gifts** through our *ministry gifts*; the Holy Spirit determines what *manifestation*, or impact, others receive from them.

Motivational	Ministry	Manifestation
Charismata Romans 12:6-8	*Diakonia* Ephesians 4:11 1 Corinthians 12:28	*Energamaton* 1 Corinthians 12:8-11
- Prophecy - Service - Teaching - Encouragement - Giving - Leadership - Mercy	- Apostles - Prophets - Evangelists - Pastor/Teacher - Teachers - Working of Miracles - Healing - Helping - Tongues - Administration/ Leadership	- Word of Wisdom - Word of Knowledge - Faith - Healing - Miracles - Prophecy - Discernment - Tongues - Interpretation of Tongues

Seven Motivational Gifts

Let's start back in Romans 12, which begins with a call to present ourselves to God as living sacrifices. Verses 4 and 5 paint a picture of the Church as a spiritual body whose members work together interdependently, just as the members of our physical body do. There's unity in that body, but it has diverse parts. We have different gifts among us (verse 6). Then Paul highlights seven specific examples:

> If your gift is *prophesying*, then prophesy in accordance with your faith; if it is *serving*, then serve; if it is *teaching*, then teach; if it is to *encourage*, then give encouragement; if it is *giving*, then give generously; if it is to *lead*, do it diligently; if it is to show *mercy*, do it cheerfully. (Romans 12:6-8, emphasis added)

With each of these phrases, the original Greek suggests that every person should focus their primary energy on their gift: "Let him serve . . ."

"Let him teach . . ." "Let him encourage . . ." In other words, "If that's your gift, then serve others in that way."

You may notice that these seven actions include behavior every believer is called to. For example, not everyone has the ***motivational gift*** of service, but we're all commanded to serve (and encourage, show mercy, give, and so on).

Furthermore, every church needs to have all the gifts at work in it. For us to grow into healthy, mature believers, we need to experience leadership, exhortation and encouragement, prophetic insight, mercy, and everything else on the list. All seven gifts need to show up in order to produce the spiritual fruit and maturity God desires. But where should you invest most of your time and energy? That varies from person to person.

Whatever your ***motivational gift*** is, focus on maximizing it, and be wise enough not to focus on gifts that aren't yours. Remember that God has prepared good works (Ephesians 2:10) for *you* to do that aren't the same as the ones He has prepared for others. You will probably be called to exercise all these functions as an act of obedience, but not necessarily with a supernatural ability. One function should stand out as the most effective and fruitful way for you to build up the Body of Christ.

There are other sets of gifts in Ephesians 4 and 1 Corinthians 12. Some of these fall in the category of "different kinds of service," and others in the category of "different kinds of workings" mentioned in 1 Corinthians 12:4-6, which I'll unpack in more detail in the next chapter.

But when you understand that you have one primary motivation that can be expressed in multiple ministries, you eliminate a lot of confusion about spiritual gifts. You experience two important "Fs"—fulfillment and fruitfulness—when you anchor yourself in your ***motivational gift***.

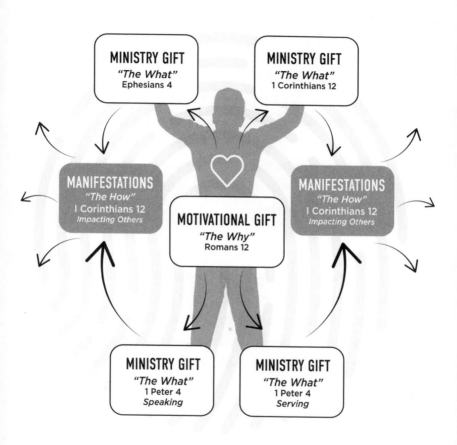

MINISTRY GIFT
"The What"
Ephesians 4

MINISTRY GIFT
"The What"
1 Corinthians 12

MANIFESTATIONS
"The How"
I Corinthians 12
Impacting Others

MOTIVATIONAL GIFT
"The Why"
Romans 12

MANIFESTATIONS
"The How"
I Corinthians 12
Impacting Others

MINISTRY GIFT
"The What"
1 Peter 4
Speaking

MINISTRY GIFT
"The What"
1 Peter 4
Serving

Note: 1 Corinthians 14 provides guidelines for the proper use of these gifts in the Church.

How Your Motivational Gift Provides Direction

Before we go into the descriptions of specific *motivational gifts*, let me give you a few examples of how they work. First is a story about a guy I've worked with for a long time named Greg. His primary *motivational gift* is *service*. He loves to serve, and he does it well. He sees needs and figures out ways to meet them.

Greg's love of people points to a *ministry gift* of *pastor/teacher*. His ability to go into an organization and smooth out relationships and get things flowing well is evidence of a *ministry gift* of *administration*. He knows both how to organize and how to help people work through problems. He counsels people all the time and has served in upper management. But he is not motivated to be a pastor.

So when people try to elevate Greg to positions of executive leadership—which is often the case—he knows how to respond: "That's not what I'm made to do. I serve by implementing other people's visions. I can help out more in a supportive role of shepherding people behind the scenes."

Greg understands that when we confuse our ***motivational gifts*** with our *ministry gifts*, we can get pulled in all sorts of directions that take us out of our primary callings. As you can imagine, this also requires great humility and self-awareness.

My wife is a second example. Theresa's ***motivational gift*** is ***exhortation***, the ability to come alongside people to comfort them and challenge them to walk more closely with the Lord. Her *ministry gifts* are *administration*, *teaching*, and *apostleship* (launching new work, for example).

She will see a need and develop an ongoing means for meeting it. She once started with a box of books and somehow built a whole library in our church, recruiting a team of several women to oversee it. More counseling happened in that library than anywhere else in our church. Her ***motivational gift*** to encourage people to walk with God paired with her *ministry gift* to coordinate and organize around that desire.

Theresa is drawn to lonely, hurting people because she sees hope for them, so she ends up mentoring many women. We once put her teaching on the radio and were flooded with requests for speaking engagements. It looked like a great opportunity for her, but she said no. She understands that she can teach as she encourages and exhorts people, but it's not her calling to be a teacher. Knowing her primary gift has helped her know when to say yes to opportunities and when to say no.

A friend named Dick is a third example. His **motivational gift** is **giving**, and it shows up in two *ministry gifts*. One of them is *apostleship*. He knows how to start things, both in the marketplace and the spiritual world. He had a senior vice president role in a very large company and then later started his own successful business because he wanted to travel less.

His business did extremely well and gave him the opportunity to exercise his ***motivational gift*** of ***giving***.

Dick became one of my mentors, and I remember sitting across the table from him after he heard about my opportunity to start a radio ministry. I had been teaching five services a weekend, and the idea of starting something new seemed crazy. But Dick saw the potential ministry impact. He launched, organized, and financed it for the first couple of years. It had nothing to do with a passion for radio; he simply recognized the possibilities and applied his primary ***motivational gift*** of ***giving*** and natural talents in business to birth Living on the Edge.

Dick also has the *ministry gift* of *helping*. As an entrepreneur with the ***motivational gift*** of ***giving***, he received many invitations to be on boards of directors and church finance committees, neither of which appealed to him at all. He's good at putting his arm around guys like me and offering much-needed advice or meeting needs through his giving. So instead of serving on boards and committees, he uses his time and money to launch ministries and help people in practical ways.

I thought for a long time that my primary ***motivational gift*** was ***leadership***, as I always found myself in leadership positions. And because one of my natural talents—even before coming to know Christ—was leading, that made sense. I discovered later that my primary ***motivational gift*** was ***prophecy***. I didn't consider that as a possibility at first because it sounded too strange. ***Leadership***, along with the *ministry gifts* of *exhortation* as a *pastor/teacher*, seemed good to me.

My motivation has always been to see lives changed and churches be what God has called them to be. That's the prophetic gift—not foretelling the future, as we commonly think of prophecy, but calling the Church into its God-given purpose, especially in the midst of cultural forces that work against that purpose. I long for the Church to have a high view of God, for pastors to walk passionately with God, and for Christians to live like Christians. That's my ***motivational gift***.

As my passion to see Christians live like Christians grew out of my ***motivational gift*** of ***prophecy***, God caused the churches I served to grow. I saw fruitfulness as I exercised the *ministry gifts* I had in areas of *teaching* and *pastoring*. God blessed the **motivational gift** of **prophecy** and the *ministry gifts* I had, and eventually I found myself leading a large congregation.

Dick and two or three elders were the ones who finally helped me see that **leadership** was not my primary **motivational gift**. They affirmed my gifts that were growing the church—studying and preaching God's Word in a culturally relevant and challenging way and offering vision for the direction of the church—but they recognized that the church had grown past my capacity to lead. In fact, I was unknowingly one of the reasons behind some problematic management issues the church was having. They gently steered me back to what I do best.

I felt liberated. I embraced the realization that God wanted me to hone my **motivational gift** of **prophecy** and focus on *pastoring, preaching,* and *teaching.* I stopped feeling pulled in directions that didn't fit my passions and zeroed in on what God had designed me to do. I had never felt such joy.

Motivational Gifts Defined

There is much to be learned about the ***motivational gifts*** listed in Romans 12:6-8 and how each gift might appear in the lives of those who have been given them. Here's an overview as a starting point for you in your discovery process.

Prophecy

> The gift of prophecy is a divine ability to proclaim God's truth with power and clarity in a timely and culturally sensitive fashion for correction, repentance, or edification— "strengthening, encouraging and comfort" (1 Corinthians 14:3).

In the Old Testament, and occasionally in the New Testament, this gift is future oriented and often predictive. But its dominant nature in any era is the ability to accurately reveal God's Word and His will. It's the consuming desire to unveil the truth of God to influence lives.

People who have this gift often intuitively ask in situations, *What went wrong here?* They have a God-given sense of what needs to happen to make it right. They recognize the culture and needs of the Church and get to the heart of the real issues that need to be addressed. Those who listen to these people can suddenly feel as though they see things clearly.

People with the prophetic ***motivational gift***

- Tend to be persuasive speakers
- Read people well
- Can come across as opinionated or insensitive
- Can depend on their speaking ability rather than on the power of the Holy Spirit if not careful

Service

The gift of service is the divine ability to attach spiritual value to accomplishing physical tasks in the Body of Christ. It's the ability to demonstrate love by meeting practical needs that facilitate other Christians in their ministry.

The word for service is *diakonia*, from which we get "deacon" and means "to wait on tables" (Acts 6:2). Even though they are often unseen, those with the gift of service are the ones who make sure everything comes together in a church's ministries. But they can be neglected in the Body of Christ.

People with this gift often intuitively ask in situations, *What can I do to help?* They have an unusual ability to detect people's needs.

People motivated with the gift of service

- Do not seek public recognition
- Are content to work behind the scenes, though they do want to know that people care
- Will often overlook their own discomfort or needs in order to serve
- Can become bitter when their hard work is not recognized

Teaching

The gift of teaching is the divine ability to understand and give a detailed explanation of biblical truth.

Teachers search out and validate truth. They love to study and can spend hours pursuing research that can shed light on our understanding of a biblical passage or event. They sometimes have a tendency to examine issues from different angles to consider many possible interpretations and focus on content to the neglect of application. They often need others around them who will shepherd hearts and help students apply the truth.

People with this gift often intuitively ask, *What is the truth on this issue? Where did you get that? Why?*

People motivated with the gift of teaching

- Love to study and do research
- Are doctrine-oriented

- May neglect the application of truth and be inattentive to needs of students
- May become proud of their knowledge

Encouragement

> The gift of encouragement is a divine ability to come alongside people and reassure, strengthen, affirm, and challenge them and stimulate faith.

The biblical word for this gift is *parakaleo*, which Jesus in John 14:16-17 used in reference to the Holy Spirit. The term is translated variously as comforter, companion, counselor, helper, or advocate.

People with this gift often intuitively ask, *What must be done to fix this? How can we move this person to wholeness?*

There are two sides to the expression of this gift. For those struggling through hard times, the encourager brings comfort, love, affirmation, and counsel. For those spinning their wheels who aren't serious about changing, the encourager becomes the exhorter, challenging people to make whatever changes are needed. Encouragers have a long fuse, but their goal is to help people become whole. They can be blunt about it when necessary.

> People motivated with the gift of encouragement/exhortation
>
> - Are gifted counselors
> - Know how to apply Scripture practically
> - Initiate, implore, and call us to godly living
> - Can spend too much time with people who want only temporary solutions
> - Might become discouraged at the lack of results

Giving

> The gift of giving is a divine ability to earn money, manage it well, and contribute wisely, cheerfully, and generously to God's work.

Givers are willing to entrust personal assets in order to support people and ministries. They are not necessarily wealthy; even in very poor communities, churches have people with this gift. Wise stewardship comes naturally to givers, and they can struggle when they see financial mismanagement.

People with this gift often intuitively ask, *What can I give to meet this need?* The answer is not always monetary, but this gift will almost always be reflected in a person's finances.

People motivated with the gift of giving

- Generally avoid the spotlight and give anonymously
- Want to know the return on their investment
- Avoid high-pressure tactics
- Might have a tendency to be prideful
- Can overemphasize material needs over spiritual needs
- Might judge others by their bank accounts

Leadership

> The gift of leadership is the divine ability to notice what needs to be done, set goals to get it done, and then attract, motivate, and lead people who can accomplish the work of the ministry.

Those with the gift of leadership enjoy responsibility. When things are disorganized or nothing is happening in an organization, they step into the gap. They see a target and envision a plan to hit it, and they recruit and coordinate people to achieve the goal. Sometimes they are so focused on the outcome of a project that they forget its purpose—for example, not just to get a building built but to love people through the ministry that will take place in it. For getting things done, they are vital to the Body of Christ.

People with this gift often intuitively ask, *What is the goal? Where are we trying to go? How do we get there?* They see ahead to the end results and can envision how to accomplish them.

People motivated with the gift of leadership

- Enjoy responsibility and taking charge
- See a need and envision a plan to meet
  the need
- Mobilize and delegate tasks to others
- Might have a tendency to use people to
  achieve their goals
- Can become proud of their power
- Sometimes forget the spiritual purpose
  behind the project

Mercy

The gift of mercy is the divine ability to
minister cheerfully and appropriately to
people who are suffering or undeserving
and to spare them the consequences they
might deserve.

People with the gift of mercy tend to be deeply
sympathetic and compassionate. With a strong
sensitivity to people's hurts and feelings, they desire
to soften the consequences (which is how God has
dealt with each of us).

They pick up on signals that other people miss, and their antennas are always up. Through their sensitive, hands-on ministry with people in need, they provide essential buffers to those with prophetic and leadership gifts by adding heavy doses of compassion to a church's ministries.

People with this gift often intuitively ask, *How can I make these people feel better?*

People motivated with the gift of mercy

- Detect and discern people's feelings
- Seek direct ministry to relieve suffering
- Provide a compassionate buffer in ministry
- Might have a hard time being firm
- Can feel that their desire to help is often misunderstood
- Might tend to resent those who don't have the gift of mercy

Responding in Your Motivational Gift

You may have heard the following helpful illustration that provides concrete examples for how each of the seven *motivational gifts* might approach a situation.

Picture seven tables at a church banquet. At each table is a representative who has one of the seven *motivational gifts*. The participants have finished their main course, and the waitstaff is beginning to clear the tables in preparation for the dessert course.

Just then, a waiter comes into the hall carrying a huge tray. Unfortunately, he collides with one of the staff cleaning up a table. He spins and falls, and the desserts on the tray go flying.

How does each of the seven representatives react to the scene?

Prophecy

Here's what the person with the gift of prophecy might say:

> *"I could see this coming from a mile away. It was a mistake from the beginning. You can't take away plates and bring dessert at the same time."*

Motivation: to correct life

Service

Here's what the person with the gift of service might say:

> *"Let me help you with that! I'll wipe you off and we'll clean up the mess together."*

Motivation: to fulfill a need

Teaching

Here's what the person with the gift of teaching might say:

> *"The real reason this happened wasn't because they were taking up plates as the dessert was being*

brought in. I've analyzed this and observed that there were seven desserts on one side of the tray and five on the other side. That threw off the waiter's balance. Furthermore, he was wearing the wrong kind of shoes, making it even more likely he would stumble and fall, ruining our desserts."

Motivation: to discover why it happened

Encouragement

Here's what the person with the gift of encouragement might say:

"I have an idea. Next time just serve the dessert with the meal."

Motivation: to correct the future

Giving

Here's what the person with the gift of giving might say:

*"The main speaker's suit jacket is ruined. Dishes
are broken and the carpet is destroyed. Here, wear
my jacket while you speak, and I'll buy you a new
suit tomorrow. And this church carpet should have
been replaced years ago. I'll throw in five thousand
dollars, and the rest of you can jump in with me."*

Motivation: To give to relieve a need

Leadership

Here's what the person with the gift of leadership
might say:

*"Jesse, find a mop. Mariel, get some paper towels.
Ben, help the waiter up. Let's have the worship
leader play one more song as we get this cleaned
up. Everyone else—we'll be ready to go in
fifteen minutes!"*

Motivation: to get back on track to accomplish
the intended goal

Mercy

Here's what the person with the gift of mercy might say:

> *"Oh, don't feel bad! This could have happened to anyone. It's okay."*

Motivation: to relieve embarrassment

Fulfillment and Fruitfulness

I believe God has given every Christian one primary ***motivational gift***, and at least one of these probably resonated with you when you read about it. Knowing which of the gifts energizes you will spare you a lot of frustration and futility.

It also will enable the Body of Christ to experience what only you can bring to it. Other believers need you to walk in the gift you've been given, and you need them to walk in theirs. This is a vital part of the process of God's masterpieces—those He is creating in your life, in the lives of those around you, and in the Body of Christ as a whole.

When you understand your primary ***motivational gift***, you will see how it plays out in various ministries in different seasons in your development. You'll also grasp how spiritual gifts operate and work together in the Church. That is how you walk in the good works God has ordained for you from before the foundation of the world. And the results are those two "Fs" I mentioned: fulfillment and fruitfulness.

Questions to Ponder

- Why is it important for Christians to discover their spiritual gifts?

- What is the difference between a person's motivational gift and ministry gift(s)?

- Think of a time when you experienced the most joy and fulfillment in serving. This might give you a clue to what your motivational gift is.

- Review the seven motivational gifts. Which one best describes your gifting?

3

Developing
YOUR SPIRITUAL GIFTS FOR THE KINGDOM

Knowing and developing your spiritual gifts is not just a nice addition to your Christian life; it's serious business. It's God's way of growing His Church and giving you a fulfilling and fruitful life and ministry.

Research has documented how important it is for each believer to operate in his or her spiritual gifts. It's crucial to the vibrancy of churches. A very famous 1996 study still referenced today found that healthy, growing churches share eight core characteristics. One of those characteristics is a spiritual gift-oriented ministry. Vibrant, effective churches train people in their giftedness and allow them to serve in it.

One of the researchers, Christian Schwarz, wrote,

> When Christians serve in their area of giftedness, they generally function less in their own strength and more in the power of the Holy Spirit. Thus ordinary people can accomplish the extraordinary![1]

Schwarz concluded that no factor influences Christians' joy and contentment as much as how they are utilizing their gifts. And no other factor has more impact on a local church community.

Five Reasons to Develop Your Spiritual Gifts

As God's workmanship, you need to understand how He has wired you. You have become a new creation in Christ Jesus, filled with His Spirit and creativity. So, how has He designed you to express who He is? How are you going to walk in the good works He has preordained for you? What are your spiritual gifts?

Here are five reasons every Christian should be eager to answer those questions.

1. Direction and purpose. You will gain clarity when you understand your key *motivational gift* clearly and the *ministry gifts* in which it operates. Your life takes on new direction and you live with a strong sense of purpose.

2. Freedom to embrace and enjoy who you are. Role models can be helpful, but the pressure you put on yourself to conform to other people's gifts and ministries keeps you from fully developing your own. When you realize you don't have to be like anybody else, you will experience wonderful, winsome, holy freedom to be the person God designed you to be.

3. Joy. When you live and work in your giftedness, there is tremendous joy in influencing lives, meeting needs, and doing the good works God has called you to do. In fact, the word for spiritual gifts, *charismata*, comes from the word for grace, which in turn comes from the word for joy.

4. *Affirmation of your victory with Christ.* You are on the winning team! Spiritual gifts are like plunder (Ephesians 4:7-8) from Christ's victory over Satan, sin, and death. Even though life in a fallen world is difficult, we have supernatural abilities as co-victors and co-heirs with Christ.

5. *Accountability.* You have been entrusted with sacred gifts and will be held responsible for their stewardship and use. This is not judgment concerning salvation; Jesus already took care of that at the cross. But one day you will stand before the judgment seat of Christ to give an account of what you did with what He gave you (2 Corinthians 5:10). You don't want to reply, "Sorry, I never figured out what mine were."

Developing Your Gifts Begins with Clarity

Several things need to happen for you to discover, develop, and deploy your spiritual gifts. An important one is clarity.

We've said that there are three categories concerning spiritual gifting (1 Corinthians 12:4-6) and that one of them is a ***motivational gift*** (listed in Romans 12:6-8). Understanding that ***motivational gift***, therefore, brings clarity to everything else we do and every other category we operate in. The Holy Spirit determines how our gifts will benefit the most people through us, and clarity aligns us with what He is doing.

Take, for example, the ***motivational gift*** of ***encouragement*** or ***exhortation***. That gift could play out in in the *ministry gift* of *apostleship*— as in starting something new, such as a counseling center—or it could show up in the *ministry gift* of *pastor/teacher*.

The effects of that ministry in the lives of others could be present via the third category (the *manifestations*) by providing knowledge, faith, or specific words of wise counsel about steps a person needs to take.

Knowing and walking in your primary motivational gift is the gateway to opening up your specific areas of ministry and fruitfulness.

Knowing and walking in your primary ***motivational gift*** is the gateway to opening up your specific areas of ministry and fruitfulness.

That's how it worked with my friend whose natural leadership skills made him a prime candidate for finance committees and boards of directors. But he was always the kind of guy who loved to learn, asked questions most of us didn't think about, and was always buying another commentary so he could understand more. In other words, he had all the signs of someone with the ***motivational gift*** of ***teaching***.

When he learned about spiritual gifts, he realized that he wasn't in the right environment for his teaching gift to flourish. His natural tendencies made him great at certain things, but he wasn't motivated by them and didn't particularly enjoy serving in those capacities.

Discovering his primary ***motivational gift*** freed him to teach, assemble a team of people (including a good leader), and build a huge Sunday school class with multiple small groups. He said he'd never experienced such joy. His teaching gift opened up wisdom, knowledge, and understanding for others. Relationships were healed and financial situations were put in order, all because my friend understood his primary ***motivational gift*** and God gave him a platform. He lived with new direction, focus, joy, and affirmation from God.

A Basic Understanding of New Testament Gifts

Understanding your primary ***motivational gift*** is essential, but it's just the beginning. To develop your *ministry gifts* and the *manifestations* of the gifts—the second and third columns of the chart that follows—you'll need a basic understanding of what each gift is and how it works. These are the arenas in which your primary ***motivational gift*** will show up in practical ways.

Motivational	Ministry	Manifestation
Charismata Romans 12:6-8	*Diakonia* Ephesians 4:11 1 Corinthians 12:28	*Energamaton* 1 Corinthians 12:8-11
- Prophecy - Service - Teaching - Encouragement - Giving - Leadership - Mercy	- Apostles - Prophets - Evangelists - Pastor/Teacher - Teachers - Working of Miracles - Healing - Helping - Tongues - Administration/ Leadership	- Word of Wisdom - Word of Knowledge - Faith - Healing - Miracles - Prophecy - Discernment - Tongues - Interpretation of Tongues

There is, of course, discussion and debate when it comes to some of the *ministry gifts* and *manifestations* we'll be looking at. God allows diversity in the Body of Christ. In my own extensive research and study, I've come to appreciate and respect different views. But for now, I'm going to share what I have learned. With Ephesians 4:11 and 1 Corinthians 12:28 as our texts, here are snapshots of the *ministry gifts* and *manifestations*.

Apostleship

> The gift of apostleship is the ability to start churches or other ministries and oversee their development.

The New Testament seems to make a distinction between the *office* of apostle and the *ministry gift*. Paul wrote that the Church was built on the foundation laid by the apostles (along with the prophets; Ephesians 2:20), referring to the twelve who were with Jesus and were eyewitnesses of His resurrection.

But several other people in the New Testament
are called apostles, generally in reference to their
ministry gifts. The word *apostle* simply means "one
who is sent," a messenger, someone who will fulfill
the purposes of the One who sent him or her.
Functioning in the *ministry gift* of apostleship often
involves ministering cross-culturally with the goal of
planting churches. I think of modern-day apostles
as the spiritual entrepreneurs of the Church.

Prophecy

> The gift of prophecy is a divine ability to
> proclaim God's truth with power and clarity
> in a timely and culturally sensitive fashion
> for correction, repentance, or edification—
> "strengthening, encouraging and comfort"
> (1 Corinthians 14:3).

As we saw in the previous chapter, prophecy can be
one of the primary **motivational gifts**. But it can
also serve as a *ministry gift*—for example, with the
motivation of exhortation or mercy.

I know a worship pastor whose primary ***motivational gift*** is mercy. His heart just goes out to people, and he is always helping those who are hurting. But when he puts together a worship set musically and artistically (he also paints), it creates an environment in which Christ is proclaimed prophetically.

Prophets are those who see the will and Word of God clearly and proclaim them. As with apostleship, there is a distinction between the office of prophet and the prophetic ministry of proclaiming God's truth for the purpose of life change. We don't get *new* revelation as biblical prophets and writers of Scripture did (as they filled the *office* of prophet), but we can still receive many biblical insights and express God's heart in specific situations (the ministry) and in fact are strongly encouraged in 1 Corinthians 14:1 to do so.

Evangelism

The gift of evangelism is the ability to effectively lead unbelievers into a saving knowledge of

Jesus. All Christians are called to have some role in evangelism, but evangelists are gifted specifically for the task.

Evangelists are motivated and empowered to share their faith with two goals: that lost people come to Christ and that other believers learn to evangelize too. Some people with this gift are most effective in personal, one-on-one, relationship-building evangelism, and others are used more in groups or large crowds, often cross-culturally.

If you don't have this gift but are around someone who does, you'll notice your compassion for lost people rising. Billy Graham attributed his impact not to his training or experience but to his heart being filled with God's overwhelming love for people who don't know Him. His passion for the lost is contagious.

I knew an elderly man who was normally very shy but was one of the greatest evangelists I've ever met. One time we got on an elevator. He immediately

introduced himself to the young woman also in
the elevator and asked her if she knew Jesus loved
her. I thought it pretty insensitive and expected
the woman to react negatively. My friend went on,
with a look of deep compassion, to share that he
had wasted half his life until Jesus had made all the
difference. Somehow that opened her up, and she
asked if it would be okay if they talked sometime.

Pastor/Teacher

> The gift of pastor/teacher provides people with
> the ability to lead, nourish, protect, and care
> for the needs of a flock of believers.

Pastor/teacher is the only dual gift in the New
Testament. It can be read as two gifts, but Paul's use
of a singular article in Ephesians 4:11 suggests that
he sees them as two aspects of the same gift.

Not everyone in the role of pastor, elder, or overseer
needs to have this gift. Some pastors operate
out of a gift of exhortation or prophecy. Every

congregation needs people who are pastor/teachers to shepherd the flock. Likewise, many with the pastor/teacher gift do not serve as pastors; they love being small-group leaders or Sunday school teachers and minister to people.

The Church needs pastor/teachers. I remember in particular one woman who taught Sunday school and mentored my daughter for several years, giving her an opportunity to develop her gifts and mature into a young woman of God. She pastored and taught her even though she wasn't officially a pastor. To shepherd, teach, and disciple is a gift God spreads through His Church to mature and love His people.

Teaching

> The gift of teaching is the divine ability to understand and give a detailed explanation of biblical truth.

The list of gifts in 1 Corinthians 12:28 overlaps

with the one in Ephesians 4:11 (beginning with apostles and prophets) but then identifies teaching as a singular gift. As we saw in the previous chapter, this can be a primary ***motivational gift***, but it's also a *ministry gift* that flows out of other ***motivational gifts*** too. Some with the *ministry gift* of teaching are motivated by exhortation, prophecy, or leadership, for example. I believe a lot of people with this gift don't see themselves as teachers but end up teaching as they live out their primary ***motivational gift***.

Miracles

> The gift of miracles is the ability to serve as an instrument of God in manifesting His supernatural power.

Miracles bear witness to God's presence and truth and often occur in association with missionary activity as a means of demonstrating who He is. The gospel message carries its own authority, of course, but God sometimes authenticates that message with miracles that open the door for the proclamation of the forgiveness of sins through Christ.

A few years ago, I was training pastors in a remote area of China. The leader of the outpost so impressed me with her compassion and tireless servanthood that I had to ask her how she learned of Christ. She told me that years earlier, her mother was dying of cancer and after all medical hope was gone, the woman heard of a Christian musician who prayed with power and offered to pray for her mother. Her mother was healed and the entire family came to faith.

In my own experience, I've seen God do miracles mostly in situations where His Word was not known and people needed a demonstration of power to grasp the reality of the gospel message. Imagine Paul walking to downtown Ephesus or Corinth and seeing a shrine to a different god on every corner. The message that Jesus is the Messiah who has been raised from the dead might not be all that remarkable or believable in that context, but some conspicuous miracles would certainly turn heads and reveal a lot about the message's truth and power.

Though God can do miraculous works through anyone, some people are particularly gifted in praying for, declaring, and seeing that kind of supernatural activity.

Healing

> The gift of healing is the ability to serve as a human instrument for God to cure illnesses and restore health.

A person with the gift of healing can't simply heal anyone they choose, but God can heal through them whenever *He* chooses. Although this healing is miraculous, it is distinct from the gift of miraculous signs and wonders that authenticated the apostles' ministries.

Healing like this was a common occurrence in the early Church. It still happens today, although we all know of many cases in which people are not healed. The New Testament tells us to pray for healing (James 5:14-15).

Some people, in reaction to false teachings about healing, swing so far in the other direction that they assume it no longer happens. But as a pastor, I've seen people anointed and healed many times, just as I've seen people not healed after being prayed for and anointed. I honestly don't know why God answers in one instance and not another. But I don't have to. I just know that God still heals and that some people are especially gifted in praying for healing.

Helping

> Helping is the ability to enhance the effectiveness of the ministry of other members of the Body.

First Corinthians 12:28 is the only place in the New Testament where the word *helping* is used, and it seems to be distinct from the gift of service. Some commentators suggest that service is group-oriented and the gift of helping is more person-oriented.

Administration/Leadership

> The gift of administration/leadership includes the ability to steer a church, ministry, or group toward the fulfillment of its goals by managing its affairs and implementing its plans.

The term used here for administration/leadership is different from the one used for the gift of leadership that we discussed earlier. Outside of Scripture, it refers to a helmsman, who steers a ship to its destination.

A person can have the gift of leadership without the gift of administration; I'm an example of that. Where the gift of leadership alone involves the ability to envision, strategize, and motivate, the gift of administration/leadership involves the ability to implement and execute big-picture plans at the operational level. Leaders ask, *What do we need to do?* Administrators/leaders ask, *How should we do this? What do we need to get there?*

People with this gift know how to plan or orchestrate and sometimes are driven a little crazy when things aren't well organized. They are vital at keeping a group, church, or organization moving toward its goals.

Wisdom

> The gift of wisdom is the ability to apply the principles of God's Word practically to specific situations and recommend the best course of action at the best time.

People with the gift of wisdom are able to turn insight and discernment into excellent advice. They usually have saturated themselves in Scripture. But wisdom is more than just biblical knowledge; it includes being able to see the chaos, problems, and struggles of life and bring the light of truth into them.

As a young pastor, I knew a man named Bill who exemplified this gift. I learned more about people, decision making, and discernment from Bill than from any seminary class. Some of the issues in my life seemed like a tangled ball of twine, but whenever I brought them to Bill, he would lay out some timeless principle that completely unraveled my tangle to where I could see what steps to take next. That's the gift of wisdom.

Knowledge

> The gift of knowledge is the ability to discover, analyze, and systematize truth for the benefit of others.

People with this gift can speak with penetrating understanding. God also may provide supernatural perception and discernment while ministering to

others, even revealing something that could not
have known by any natural means. A "word of
knowledge" can be helpful in pointing out a good
biblically acceptable direction or insight that could
not be obtained through general counsel.

Sometimes this gift can be misused, with people
claiming knowledge that's really just a guess. It
can be abused too, such as when people issue
supposedly divine directives (for example, "God
told me you're to leave your wife, take this job,
move to this city . . ."). But we have to be careful
not to throw the baby out with the bathwater in our
understanding of some gifts.

Once when I was a young Christian, I was at the
beach reading my Bible, enjoying good fellowship
with friends, praying and thinking, watching the
sunset, and sensing God's warm and encouraging
presence as if I could just reach out and touch
Him. Far down the beach was a guy walking in
our direction, and a very clear thought came into
my mind: *This man is a homosexual, and he is going*

to come and sit down by you. I want you to tell him about Me.

I wondered if I was just making it up, but sure enough, the guy came closer, got to the edge of the area where I was sitting, and turned toward me and sat down nearby. His eyes were red. And because God had prepared me, I knew how to respond when he said, "I just broke up with my life partner and noticed you had a Bible here. I just need somebody to talk to." Forty-five minutes later, we both prayed, and he received Christ as his Savior.

I don't know how it works, but I do know the gift of knowledge exists to reach people, not impress them. God sometimes chooses to give very clear knowledge of a situation in advance, and certain people are gifted at receiving it and acting on it.

Faith

> The gift of faith is the ability to have a vision for what God wants done and confidently

believe that it will be accomplished regardless of whatever circumstances and obstacles seem to be in the way.

The gift of faith transforms vision into reality. Sometimes it's stirred up by someone else's *motivational gift*, such as responding with unusual faith to a message from a pastor, teacher, or prophet.

Years ago, a woman was listening to me on the radio. She had been sick for a long time. Her treatments were ineffective, and the medical community was stumped. In the closing prayer of the broadcast, I made a comment about believing that God is sovereign and still answers big prayers. The woman said that in that moment, God gave her faith to believe. The next day, she went to the doctor and all her symptoms were gone.

It might help to pause for just a moment to remember how God uses our gifts in the Body of Christ. I used my *motivational gift* of *prophecy* to proclaim God's Word. Others used their *ministry gifts* of *administration/leadership* to put that message on the radio. And the *manifestation* (impact) was the *gift of faith* that resulted in supernatural healing.

Some people are particularly gifted in embracing faith, calling it forth in those around them, and seeing God do amazing things through it.

Discernment

> The gift of discernment is the ability to discern the spirit of truth from the spirit of error.

God gives all of us the ability to discern truth when we soak our minds and hearts in Scripture, but some people have the gift of a special sensitivity in recognizing counterfeits, false teachings, demonic influence, and carnal motives.

It's therefore important for those with discernment to be listened to by decision makers. When a church or an organization is aligning people for certain tasks and responsibilities, partnering with other ministries, or making any other decision that creates a partnership with another entity, you want someone to be able to sense whether things are being done for the right reasons and with the right motives. The gift of discernment does that.

Tongues

> Tongues is the ability to receive and impart a spiritual message in a language that the recipient has never learned so that others in the Body can be edified.

In a ministry setting, the *interpretation of tongues* is necessary; the message should be interpreted either by the recipient or someone else with the gift of interpretation.

This is perhaps the most controversial gift, and opinions on it vary widely[2], but the way Paul dealt with it in 1 Corinthians 14 tells us that he saw this gift as important but potentially disruptive if not handled with care. In Corinth, some people were apparently using it to draw attention to themselves—always an abuse when exercising spiritual gifts. At its best, the gift of interpretation demonstrates God's power and reveals His message to people who would not otherwise understand it.

Those are brief snapshots of each of the *ministry gifts* and *manifestations*. You will want to explore some more teachings on the ones you think might be yours.

To Develop Gifts, You Must Exercise Them

Once you have recognized your primary **motivational gift**, you can identify how these *ministry gifts* and *manifestations* operate in your life and then learn to develop them more.

You can't learn how to swim by just reading about the breaststroke; you have to get in the water. The same is true with developing an understanding of and cultivating your spiritual gifts. You must exercise them in several arenas of growth. The following are four levels of exploration to consider.

1. Involvement in people's lives and needs.
Spiritual gifts are about loving people. You need to get involved in their lives. It's fine if you don't know exactly which gifts God has equipped you with. Sign up for a church ministry on a temporary basis and, after about three months, pray and evaluate your experience. Just start somewhere, and you'll be amazed at how God takes one step of faith in that direction to lead you into the ministry He has for you.

2. Involvement in a small-group community.
God designed spiritual gifts as a way for Him to touch others through you. That same presence, power, and love that Christ brought into your life can flow outward to others—but only if you're in the midst of some meaningful relationships. Attending church occasionally, or even just online, is a start, but you need a community of people who know you and are committed to authentically doing life with one

another. In that context, your spiritual gifts will be identified, confirmed, and practiced.

3. Involvement in ongoing training and education. Think of your spiritual gifts as muscles. God gives you big, little, and medium-sized muscles, but they get stronger and better only through exercise. You need time, maturity, and ongoing training, practice, and feedback. If you have the gift of teaching, for example, you need to teach to develop your gift. You also need to read and study. I almost always listen to great teachers when I'm in my car, first to learn and ask God how He wants me to respond, and second to understand what makes that teacher a great communicator. The only way we develop this gift is to learn from other people, and it works the same way with other spiritual gifts too. You dig in and enter into a training process.

4. Involvement in regular risk-taking opportunities. You can read books, listen to audio, study, analyze charts of spiritual gifts, and speculate

about which ones God has given you, but nothing is going to come of them until you jump in. You may be very nervous about it at first—most people are—but it will always come down to jumping in with both feet. Just get involved in a ministry where you think you'll fit best, start loving people there, and do what you feel passionate about doing. You can readjust later if you need to, but you'll be growing stronger and experiencing a lot of joy in the process.

That's how you become a paintbrush in the hand of the Master, dipping into His brilliant palette of grace and adding your own colors to the grand masterpiece. You will see people's lives change, including your own, and become part of God's extreme makeover. Nothing will match the joy and fulfillment that comes with doing what He made you to do and walking in the good works He has prepared for you (Ephesians 2:10).

Questions to Ponder

- You just finished reading a long list of definitions of spiritual gifts. What did you learn that was new?

- What do you think your motivational gift is? What one or two ministry gifts and manifestations do you think you might have as well?

- What are the five reasons for developing your spiritual gifts? Can you think of any others?

- Developing your spiritual gifts means getting involved with people. Where could you use your gifts that would get you involved in others' lives? Who could help you get started?

4

Warning!
BEWARE OF
SPIRITUAL-GIFT ABUSE

God gives spiritual gifts to demonstrate His nature through His people and change lives for all eternity. That's a powerful dynamic in which the Holy Spirit shows up in the lives of believers to bring forth supernatural work and fruitfulness. The stakes are high. But in anything that involves that much power, there is also the potential for it to be distorted or abused.

Let's take a look at ten common signs of abuse and misuse of spiritual gifts.

1. *When spiritual gifts are used to manipulate or exert power or control in relationships.*

Spiritual gifts are "given for the common good" (1 Corinthians 12:7). They are meant to build people up and turn the focus on God rather than on the people using them. Personal control and manipulation are always signs that abuse of the gifts is occurring.

I experienced this as a young Christian when a woman I hardly knew told me that God would not use my life if Theresa and I got married. God can certainly use other people to express concern about situations in our lives, but when a major decision has already been covered in prayer, counsel, and careful consideration before the Lord, He probably isn't going to speak through a lone, unknown voice like that. It stirred up confusion, doubt, and guilt over something I had already discerned as God's will.

Those feelings are hallmarks of ungodly manipulation and not how spiritual gifts are meant to work. When someone says, "God told me you're supposed to . . . ," it's not a good sign.

2. When someone claims to be able to impart a specific gift if you follow a formula. The
Holy Spirit gives gifts "just as he determines" (1 Corinthians 12:11). Gifts can be imparted (Romans 1:11), but not by independent human will or formulaic responses.

I remember as a young Christian going to a meeting and being told that if I went into a specific room, I was "guaranteed" to receive a particular gift. The peer pressure was overwhelming; the manipulation was intense.

So, when someone seems to be taking on the role of the Holy Spirit and promising a particular gift if you follow their instructions—and implying that you don't have enough faith if the instructions don't work—beware!

3. When a gift is treated as universal evidence of spirituality, salvation, or a unique spiritual blessing. The questions in 1 Corinthians 12:29-30 ("Are all apostles? Are all prophets? . . . Do all speak in tongues? Do all interpret?") are rhetorical questions with an implied answer of no. In other words, no one has all the gifts, and no gift is given to all. Gifts are not tied in the New Testament to evidence of salvation or sanctification; they are given for ministry. Not knowing or experiencing your gifts yet does not mean you have less of God; it simply means this is an area of growth for you.

4. When the focus of a church service or ministry event is on the manifestation of spiritual gifts rather than on the Giver and His purposes for the Church. Having a service or event promoting miracles and other dramatic activity can sweep people into a blind emotional reaction or even a frenzy and turn into a show rather than accomplishing any real ministry that transforms lives. The purpose of the gifts is "to equip his people for works of service, so that the body of Christ may be built up" (Ephesians 4:12). When the focus is on the leader and the gifts, the potential for abuse is high.

5. *When you compare your spiritual gifts with others' gifts.* It is in our nature to compare ourselves with others—I've done it in ministry situations at times—but Paul's metaphor of the human body in 1 Corinthians 12:12-26 demonstrates how futile that tendency is. It would be silly for a foot to be jealous of a hand, or an ear to wish it were an eye. All the parts are needed for the body to work. When we wish we had someone else's gifts, we end up striving in our own strength rather than depending on the Holy Spirit. And if we think our own gifts are better than someone else's, we become driven by pride. In 2 Corinthians 10:12, Paul warned against measuring ourselves against others. Doing so never leads to spiritual fruitfulness.

6. *When any extreme position on spiritual gifts is taught as the singular right interpretation.* At one end of the spectrum, some people believe (or act as if) spiritual gifts don't exist. At the other end, some believe that a truly Spirit-filled Christian will have all of them. The first group sees disunity and abuses and wants nothing to do with the gifts, and the second equates operating in all the gifts with Christlikeness.

There may be times when you don't overtly see spiritual gifts operating in your life, and there may be other times when gifts that aren't normally yours come to life to help you meet specific needs. Scripture teaches clearly that the gifts are real and apportioned as the Holy Spirit chooses, which means you have some but not all. Walk closely with Jesus and He will direct your path in the timing and use of your gifts (Psalm 32:8).

7. When you use your spiritual gifts in your own strength or put them to use to impress others or satisfy your ego. God doesn't take away the tool when you're using it the wrong way. He will honor His gift. But when we operate a gift using our own strength rather than the power of the Spirit, the result is not good. This is especially tempting in the "up front" gifts, such as leadership, teaching, exhortation, and prophecy. A person in a visible role can get carried away with the attention that comes with it. Yet none of those gifts works smoothly and effectively when the less visible gifts aren't at work in the ministry too.

By contrast, some people with those behind-the-scenes gifts are often tempted to envy the more visible ones, to want to be somebody and feel important. All Christians need to understand that they *already* are "somebody" in Christ and that every gift is on equal footing. Then they live out their callings with that understanding.

8. When you observe a person with a spiritual gift and assume he or she is spiritually mature. Spiritual maturity is a life marked by the fruit of the Spirit as described in Galatians 5:22-23 ("love, joy, peace, forbearance, kindness, goodness, faithfulness, gentleness and self-control"). Spiritual gifts are God's means to help us move toward producing fruit in our lives—in other words, becoming more Christlike.

So, if a brother or sister dazzles you with an amazing spiritual gift, praise God, but don't conclude that just because He is using the person in that way, he or she has reached some higher level of spiritual maturity. God's purpose is to draw us into deeper love and discipleship.

9. *When apparent manifestations of the Spirit are counterfeited by human schemes or demonic forces.* Don't assume that all miracles are a work of God. Many will be—it's a mistake to live skeptically and dismiss miracles as counterfeits—but it's important to be discerning.

Jesus acknowledged the possibility of people doing miracles in His name without following Him as Lord and of false messiahs performing unholy signs and wonders (Matthew 24:24).

I've known people who have gone completely in the other direction and rejected all miracles as deceptive, and clearly that's not the case. But if you see miracles without the fruit of the Spirit or in support of a minister's personal wealth and fame, those are huge warning signs.

10. *When a Christian community teaches that the discovery, development, and deployment of spiritual gifts is optional.* Spiritual gifts are not items on a buffet. Jesus won a cosmic victory over sin and the powers of darkness, proclaimed that victory in hell (1 Peter 3:19), and gave gifts to human beings as plunder

> When we treat spiritual gifts casually, we devalue the power of that victory in our own lives.

(Ephesians 4:7-8). Like a conquering king, He stripped the enemy of power and took captives. When we treat spiritual gifts casually, we devalue the power of that victory in our own lives.

Diligently discovering, developing, and deploying our gifts honors Jesus. It also prepares us to stand before God's judgment seat with a positive account of our discipleship and receive His rewards (2 Corinthians 5:9-10). We become responsible stewards of God's investment in us.

Staying Spiritually Healthy

Some people run from spiritual gifts, but that's the wrong response. We instead need to be aware of potential problems and abuses as we move forward with action plans for implementing them. If a warning light on your car's dashboard comes on, you know something is not as it should be. Likewise, with spiritual gifts, you also need to pay attention to warning signs that can alert you that something is wrong and then take the appropriate, wise steps for staying spiritually healthy and strong in your service of the Lord.

Questions to Ponder

- Which of the spiritual-gift abuses or misuses have you observed occurring or experienced yourself?

- What precautions can you and your community take to make sure you don't fall into any of these abuses?

- Prior to this study, how would you have described your attitude toward spiritual gifts: Casual? Mildly interested? Passionate?

- What one specific step are you going to take to better discover, develop, and deploy your spiritual gifts in order to love God's people and glorify Christ Jesus?

CONCLUSION

We've looked at how spiritual gifts work in a believer's life, introduced the characteristics of each one, and discussed some potential abuses and misuses. Now it's time for you to develop an action plan for using your spiritual gifts. Whether you are just discovering which ones are yours or developing some you've ministered with for years, you need a strategy for deploying them for maximum fruitfulness.

Your Spiritual-Gift Action Plan

I believe that if you take the following seven steps, you will grow dramatically in the spiritual gifts God has given you.

*1. **Commit*** to discovering, deploying, and developing your spiritual gifts in your local church. Think of it as a spiritual contract, a binding agreement: *Lord, if You show me my gifts, I'll do whatever it takes to learn to use them.* God responds to that commitment faithfully.

*2. **Pray*** seriously, seeking divine guidance. God loves you and promises to answer your prayers. He wants to show you this. Jesus said that if you seek, you will find. Pray daily to grow in your gifts.

*3. **Study*** the gift passages in God's Word: Romans 12:4-8, 1 Corinthians 12, Ephesians 4:11-13, and 1 Peter 4:10-11. Read some commentaries and dig into the meanings of these passages. God will reveal the truth in increasingly deeper ways.

4. Seek good counsel. Talk to spiritually mature people who know you and will speak truth to you. Notice what people affirm in you. Eventually, a pattern will emerge that points you in the direction of your gifts.

5. Test the waters for a few weeks or months. Try different gifts on for size. You may discover that some aren't a fit for you, and that's fine. As you minister to others, you will be drawn into the areas where you are most effective.

6. Examine the fulfillment factor. This is not the same as the "easy" factor. In fact, exercising your spiritual gifts may be very difficult at times. But look for what kind of ministry flows from you and how fulfilling it is. In what ministry activities do you especially feel God's pleasure?

7. Recognize God's evident blessing. Your fulfillment is one of the two "Fs" of spiritual gifts; fruitfulness is the other. Your gifts will not necessarily change lives overnight, but God will use you to influence other people.

For the Church and for the Watching World

You are God's workmanship. He has created you in Christ Jesus. He has prepared wonderful works for you to walk in. And those works will be largely determined by the supernatural endowments given to you by Jesus, activated by the Holy Spirit, in alignment with God's Word, so that God's glory and the preeminence of Christ is exalted.

It's a beautiful thing when that happens, not only for you and for the Church but also for a watching world that wonders whether God is real and if Christianity is true.

You are one of God's masterpieces who demonstrates who He is. As you learn to discover, develop, and then deploy your spiritual gifts, you'll find there is nothing more satisfying than the gifts of His Spirit flowing through your life!

NOTES

1 Christian Schwarz, Natural Church Development:
A Guide to Eight Essential Qualities of Healthy
Churches (Carol Stream, IL: ChurchSmart Resources,
1996), 26. The classic major empirical study involved
hundreds of churches of all sizes around the world
from a wide spectrum of Christian denominations
and beliefs.

2 There is considerable debate on tongues as a corporate
gift to be used in a church gathering and as a private
gift used in prayer. That discussion is beyond the scope
of this book. You'll find some helpful resources on this
topic in the following bibliography. In addition, I speak
on this topic in my teaching series, "The Holy Spirit:
Experiencing His Power and Presence 24/7," which is
available at livingontheedge.org.

SELECTED BIBLIOGRAPHY

Barclay, William. *The Letter to the Corinthians*. 2nd ed. Philadelphia: Westminster, 1975.

Barclay, William. *The Letter to the Romans*. 2nd ed. Philadelphia: Westminster, 1975.

Barclay, William. *The Letters to the Galatians and Ephesians*. 2nd ed. Philadelphia: Westminster, 1975.

Boa, Ken. *Conformed to His Image: Biblical, Practical Approaches to Spiritual Formation*. Grand Rapids, MI: Zondervan, 2001.

Bridge, Donald, and David Phypers. *Spiritual Gifts and the Church*. Downers Grove, IL: InterVarsity, 1973.

Brown, Colin, ed. *The New International Dictionary of New Testament Theology*. Vols. 1–3. Regency Reference Library. Grand Rapids, MI: Zondervan, 1975.

Bruce, F. F. *Romans*. Tyndale New Testament Commentaries. 2nd ed. Grand Rapids, MI: Eerdmans, 1985.

Bugbee, Bruce. *What You Do Best in the Body of Christ: Discover Your Spiritual Gifts, Personal Style, and God-Given Passion*. Grand Rapids, MI: Zondervan, 1995.

Cranfield, C. E. B. *The Epistle to the Romans*. International Critical Commentary. Vol. 2. Edinburgh, Scotland: T&T Clark, 1979.

Deere, Jack. *The Beginner's Guide to the Gift of Prophecy*. Ventura, CA: Regal, 2001.

Foulkes, Francis. *Ephesians*. Tyndale New Testament Commentaries. 2nd ed. Grand Rapids, MI: Eerdmans, 1989.

Friedrich, Gerhard, ed. *Theological Dictionary of the New Testament*. Vols. 1–10. Translated by Geoffrey W. Bromiley. Grand Rapids, MI: Eerdmans, 1964.

Gaebelein, Frank E. *The Expositor's Bible Commentary*. Vols. 10–11. Grand Rapids, MI: Zondervan, 1978.

Gingrich, F. Wilbur. *Shorter Lexicon of the Greek New Testament*. Chicago: University of Chicago Press, 1965.

Grosheide, F. W. *The First Epistle to the Corinthians*. New International Commentary on the New Testament. Grand Rapids, MI: Eerdmans, 1953.

Hendriksen, William. *Galatians and Ephesians*. New Testament Commentary. Grand Rapids, MI: Baker, 1967 (Ephesians), 1968 (Galatians).

Hendriksen, William. *Paul's Epistle to the Romans*. New Testament Commentary. Grand Rapids, MI: Baker, 1981.

McRae, William J. *The Dynamics of Spiritual Gifts*. Grand Rapids, MI: Zondervan, 1976.

Metzger, Bruce M. *Lexical Aids for Students of New Testament Greek*. Princeton, NJ: self-published, 1977.

Morris, Leon. *1 Corinthians*. Tyndale New Testament Commentaries. 2nd ed. Grand Rapids, MI: Eerdmans, 1985.

Rees, Erik. *S.H.A.P.E.: Finding and Fulfilling Your Unique Purpose for Life*. Grand Rapids, MI: Zondervan, 2006.

Rienecker, Fritz, *A Linguistic Key to the Greek New Testament*. Vol. 1 (Matthew–Acts). Translated by Cleon L. Rogers Jr. Grand Rapids, MI: Zondervan, 1976.

Wigram, George V. *The Englishman's Greek Concordance of the New Testament.* 3rd ed. Grand Rapids, MI: Zondervan, 1970.

Wuest, Kenneth S. *Wuest's Word Studies from the Greek New Testament.* Vol. 1. Grand Rapids, MI: Eerdmans, 1973.

STUDY THE BIBLE
with Chip

Daily Discipleship: True Spirituality is a 17-day journey exploring Romans 12 that will help you learn how to build five core relationships, understand five true biblical expectations, and answer life's biggest questions.

Each day, I'll share a short teaching video, which I promise will never run longer than 10 minutes. Then I'll ask you to invest 10 more minutes of your own time on a simple follow-up assignment.

Let me help you develop the habit of studying the Bible and applying it to every part of your life. I hope you'll join me.

BIBLE STUDIES by
CHIP INGRAM

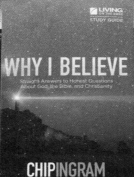

Available at LivingontheEdge.org

Also Available
THE CHIP INGRAM APP

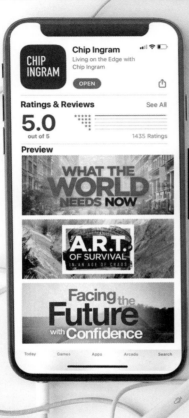

Life-Changing Truth to Help You Grow Closer to God